LIGHT UNLOCKED

Light Unlocked

CHRISTMAS CARD POEMS

Edited by
KEVIN CROSSLEY-HOLLAND
&
LAWRENCE SAIL

with engravings by
JOHN LAWRENCE

ENITHARMON PRESS

First published in 2005
by Enitharmon Press
26B Caversham Road
London NW5 2DU

www.enitharmon.co.uk

Distributed in the UK by
Central Books
99 Wallis Road
London E9 5LN

Distributed in the USA and Canada
by Dufour Editions Inc.
PO Box 7, Chester Springs
PA 19425, USA

Reprinted November 2005

ISBN 1 904634 18 4 (hardback)

Enitharmon Press gratefully acknowledges the financial support of Arts
Council England, London.

British Library Cataloguing-in-Publication Data.
A catalogue record for this book is available
from the British Library.

*

The anthology's title is
derived from Richard Burns's
poem 'Dawn' (page 52).

Typeset in Garamond by Servis Filmsetting Ltd
and printed in England by
Antony Rowe Ltd

Contents

5

Foreword

Light Unlocked brings together poems sent by their authors as Christmas greetings: and the anthology's starting point is really the simple fact that both of us have, over the years, received and sent them. This angle of approach – poems at Christmas rather than necessarily about Christmas – has meant that from the outset we could not know the exact range of subject matter and mood which our quest for eligible poems might reveal. It has been rewarding to discover their breadth and variety. Here are summers as well as winters, not only angels but birds (a whole parliament of fowls), the sea as well as Santa, evocations of the Orkneys and Slovakia alongside Bethlehem.

Certain themes recur, in addition to the notation of time and the festival of Christmas. For many of these writers, Christmas seems to be a chance to take stock of the world's dole, to celebrate a vivid instance of the natural world, or to consider the earth in the context of the cosmos or the lesser orbits of our consumer society. As for seasonal weather, it would seem that snow has not yet been displaced by global warming.

When it comes to Christmas itself, both the religious and secular markers of the occasion have found their place. On the one hand, Advent, the Annunciation, Christmas Eve, the Slaughter of the Innocents, the visit of the Magi: on the other, good cheer, eating and drinking, Christmas circulars, Boxing Day (unless you think of it solely as St Stephen's Day), New Year's Eve. In either case, the poet thinking to write about Christmas faces the same challenge, to rework ground already poached and to make something new of images and incidents flattened by familiarity.

We are grateful to John Lawrence for his compact yet expansive engravings which, to our minds, perfectly capture the essence of our anthology and, indeed, the spirit of Christmas. We also thank authors and publishers alike for allowing us to print or reprint poems: and we're especially indebted to Stephen Stuart-Smith, of Enitharmon, for his unfailing perceptiveness and patience.

We hope that readers will derive as much enjoyment from the anthology as we have had in compiling it.

KEVIN CROSSLEY-HOLLAND and LAWRENCE SAIL

HOUSE OF WINTER

At last, the house of winter. Find
On the sill
Intricate ice jewellery, a snowflake.

Open one dark door. Flame-flung,
A golden moth! Soon
A candle flame, tranquil and tall.

It is a bitter house. On the step
Birds starve.
In the cellar, the poor have only
    words to warm them.

Inside one chamber, see
A bare thorn.
Wait. A bud breaks. It is a white rose.

We think, in the heart of the house
A table is set
With a wine jar and broken bread.

GEORGE MACKAY BROWN

THE CHRISTMAS LIFE

'If you don't have a real tree, you don't bring the Christmas life into the house.' Josephine Mackinnon, aged 8

Bring in a tree, a young Norwegian spruce,
Bring hyacinths that rooted in the cold.
Bring winter jasmine as its buds unfold –
Bring the Christmas life into this house.

Bring red and green and gold, bring things that shine,
Bring candlesticks and music, food and wine.
Bring in your memories of Christmas past.
Bring in your tears for all that you have lost.

Bring in the shepherd boy, the ox and ass,
Bring in the stillness of an icy night,
Bring in a birth, of hope and love and light.
Bring the Christmas life into this house.

WENDY COPE

SUMMER TIME ENDS

How nice looking up, some cloudy afternoon,
To see that what has fallen suddenly
Is twilight, and an earlier chance to draw
The curtains while you have the energy.

Now everything falls, go down with it and give
Yourself to the gravity, putting up a show
Of warming wistfulness with the last leaves.
Fall hard, and stay there, waiting for the snow.

The nights are drawing in, nothing wrong with that.
The poet says: *Darkness cures what day inflicts.*
It is as normal to welcome winter back
As to loathe the spring. Popular interdicts

May forbid that preference, but snow walks are like
Illicit love with no one else betrayed;
Are like the joy, as you step out through the white,
Of the first alligator in the first everglade.

Harden your skin, then, for the rigorous spell
Between October and the April days
When the clocks go wrong again. Live for the thought
Of the bracing dark and the heavenly displays,

On frosty nights, of dotty groups of stars
You may sit and try to specify all night
– As if there were no tomorrow to dissolve
Their shining in dull anywheres of light.

ALAN BROWNJOHN

SNOW

I have as many ways
of saying I am sorry
as an Eskimo has
of explaining snow

often the windows
seem to leave
the sunlight out of sight,
its red glow
like a ghost
that has passed without
looking in

it is an experience
which speaks only
from hollow to hollow:
a room
where someone has been
or may arrive

where I could learn to sit
cross-legged with sorrow
as a mantra:
an anticipation
of love
that time and only time
may describe.

EDWIN BROCK

ADVENT CALENDAR

He will come like last leaf's fall.
One night when the November wind
has flayed the trees to bone, and earth
wakes choking on the mould,
the soft shroud's folding.

He will come like frost.
One morning when the shrinking earth
opens on mist, to find itself
arrested in the net
of alien, sword-set beauty.

He will come like dark.
One evening when the bursting red
December sun draws up the sheet
and penny-masks its eye to yield
the star-snowed fields of sky.

He will come, will come,
will come like crying in the night,
like blood, like breaking,
as the earth writhes to toss him free.
He will come like child.

ROWAN WILLIAMS

15

WINGS

Whether or not they are of angels
Or just the makeshift would-be
Of human flight from humdrum
To grace, theirs is a sudden restlessness
On buoyant shoulders, an uplift
Aimed at joy and making it.
So for every earthbound thought
There's the counter-weight,
A grief that covers its face in shame
Then rises with the season
As if from sleep, unfolding wings
To journey through the brightness of the air.

JOHN MOLE

CAROL OF THE BIRDS

Feet that could be clawed but are not . . .
Arms that might have flown but did not . . .
No one said 'Let there be angels!' but the birds

Whose choirs fling alleluias over the sea,
Herring gulls, black backs carolling raucously
While cormorants dry their wings on a rocky stable.

Plovers that stoop to sanctify the land
And scoop small, roundy mangers in the sand,
Swaddle a saviour each in a speckled shell.

A chaffinchy fife unreeling in the marsh
Accompanies the tune a solo thrush
Half sings, half talks in riffs of wordless words,

As hymns flare up from tiny muscled throats,
Robins and hidden wrens whose shiny notes
Tinsel the precincts of the winter sun.

What loftier organ than these pipes of beech,
Pillars resounding with the jackdaws' speech,
And poplars swayed with light like shaken bells?

Wings that could be hands, but are not . . .
Cries that might be pleas but cannot
Question or disinvent the stalker's gun,

Be your own hammerbeam angels of the air
Before, in the maze of space, you disappear,
Stilled by our dazzling anthrocentric mills.

ANNE STEVENSON

CHRISTMAS CIRCULARS

This is the season when the myth-makers
play Holy Families – their filtered lives
appropriately merging with the stream
of set Nativities, Madonnas, doves . . .

'Robert has been promoted yet again!
We're all extremely proud of him, although
it means he has to travel quite a lot.
Sam's football-mad, but passed his Grade 5 oboe.

Jean took an evening class, Renaissance art
– meals in the oven, but we were amazed
at all she knew on our super stay in Rome.
Beth triumphed in GCSE – six As!'

And from the emigrés: 'We came in June . . .
appalled at how run-down England's become
– no really open space . . . how did we stand
the weather all those years we lived in Brum?

We have a lovely place near Armidale.
Kate is the tennis champion of her school.
You wouldn't know us, we're so brown – think of us
all celebrating Christmas round the pool!'

They say, between the lines where they regret
there isn't time to write to each of us:
Our life is an accomplishment, a pearl
whose perfect shape and sheen deserve applause.

It's hard, of course. But when we see our lives
reflected here, we're almost led to think
that that's reality. So though poor Jean's
on Prozac for her nerves, and Robert drinks,

and though the children quarrel constantly
and Kate won't eat, and sometimes wets the bed,
and though we often seem to feel the draught
knife through well-fitting doors – it can't be said.

CAROLE SATYAMURTI

18

COCK ROBIN AND CUTTY WREN

'What's under the sky?' Says Billow to Bellow.
'What's under the sky?' Says Bluster to Blow.
The sky is plucking the winter goose,
What's under the sky is snow.

'What's under the snow?' Says Shiver to Shudder.
'What's under the snow?' Says Chatter to Chill.
The snow is tucking the world up tight,
What's under the snow is hill.

'What's under the hill?' Says Colder to Moulder.
'What's under the hill?' Says Gristle to Grave.
The hill is nursing its hollow heart,
What's under the hill is cave.

'What's in the cave?' Says Wrinkle to Rankle.
'What's in the cave?' Says Wretched to Wrong.
The cave is filled with what can't be killed,
What's in the cave is song.

'Who sings the song?' Says Stricken to Sicken.
'Who sings the song?' Says Wither to Wan.
The King and Queen of the Shining Year:
Cock Robin and Cutty Wren.

'To battle! To battle!' Shouts Shiver to Shudder.
'To battle! To battle!' Shouts Chatter to Chill.
They waged the war all winter long . . .
But the song is swelling still
In the hollow of the hill.

HUGH LUPTON

19

'I FEEL THE RUSH OF GABRIEL'S WINGS'

I feel the rush of Gabriel's
wings, the shock that he should kneel,

the whispered question. I sing prayers
into myself, share my days, my fears

with him, helpless master, unmade maker,
God and man, my son and father,

Carried in me, weightless, faceless,
Lord of life, of seas, skies, stars.

MICHAEL SYMMONS ROBERTS

20

THE ANNUNCIATION

Tintoretto

This is no swallow, no butterfly.
Feathered with Concorde power
Titanic bulk, breathlessly aerobic
Gabriel dives in under the lintel.
Wings swept back behind Olympic shoulders,
he tilts like a display pilot
and just clears the entrance.

Mary pulls up under the impact,
cherubs sail on the draught
like a herd of sky-diving babies. Outside
Joseph grapples with a bit
of four-by-two, oblivious to the super-human
frequency. The earth's in a bad way.

As to Gabriel
you can see he's not going to help
pick up the pieces, he's not even going to land.
Message delivered on a rush of air,
no buttering up of Mary,
his beautiful arms poised towards heaven
before he back-flips out of there.

RHIAN GALLAGHER

21

THE GLIMMERING

The horizon draws the line
at having been tamped down
all through a slutchy autumn,
moves in as a caul
of rain which blears the hills,
hissing like the prefix which history
adds to words and laughter:
finally, shrinks to the glimmering
from under a stable door,
a straw-breadth of light which can only
imply the warmth of spring
or the memory of it – the long
pursed buds of the lily
peeling open on the angel's wand.

LAWRENCE SAIL

FRAGMENT

One of those Autumn days
the light gets everything just right,
when crisper focus is unthinkable
and colours are absolute
about what colours want to be:

this common beech
on the cusp between green and brown,
brown's crux of desire,
green's determined surrender.

MATT SIMPSON

PAGES FROM 'A SUSSEX CALENDAR'

January   month of the little owls
fifty years ago, that screamed from the oak-trees.
Wind wrapped its beard round our house.
In the interval I kept still.

February   month of the moon, firecracker
to a bound garden of frozen debris.
Vegetables given over to icicles. Black
canes and luminous gravel.

...

April   my mother's month of seedlings,
of plantings, nurslings, dandlings, in her walk
the firm wrenching of the first dandelions.
The fox who trots to her.

May   phlox and sweet william and wallflower.
Grape leaves in their green nascence. Birds
as loud as grapeshot, great divas in the fringe
theatres of the spinneys.

June   month of the four noble flower-beds.
Each summer they set out kings and queens,
deep tiger lily, dark iris, red rose, amaryllis,
a chess played slowly.

...

August   month of my sticky birthday,
chocolate ice-cream and a tide of shingle
that bounced off my blue ankles: the waves
my mother dared us into.

...

December   my Dada, Father Christmas,
his rouged nose and white wool beard,
'I'm an old old man, come a long long way'.
After the gifts he flies.

JUDITH KAZANTZIS

24

THE DADA CHRISTMAS CATALOGUE

Chocolate comb
Can-of-worms opener
Non-stick frying pan
Two sticky frying pans
Book end
Abrasive partridges
Inflatable fridge
Set of nervous door handles
Overnight tea-bag
Instant coffee table
Pair of non-secateurs
Mobile phone-booth
Underwater ashtray
13 amp bath plug
Pair of socks, identical but for the colour
Box of Tunisian (past their sell-by) dates
See-through elastoplasts
Nasal floss (unwaxed)
Contact lens adhesive
Canteen of magnetic cutlery
Three-way mirror

Not a pipe.

ROGER McGOUGH

THE STONE HARE

Think of it waiting three hundred million years,
not a hare hiding in the last stand of wheat,
but a premonition of stone, a moonlit reef
where corals reach for the light through clear

waters of warm Palaeozoic seas.
In its limbs lie the story of the earth,
the living ocean, then the slow birth
of limestone from the long trajectories

of starfish, feather-stars, crinoids and crushed shells
that fill with calcite, harden, wait for the quarryman,
the timed explosion and the sculptor's hand.
Then the hare, its eye a planet, springs from the chisel

to stand in the grass, moonlight's muscle and bone,
the stems of sea-lilies slowly turned to stone.

GILLIAN CLARKE

CHRISTMAS HOLIDAY

In the december graveyard blossom moved
against remembering stone, softer than snow.
Along the christmas river we surprised
buds in the act of daring, sweet as toffee;
fields lay stretched and steaming in the sun,
and smoke was neat as feathers on the sky.
But discandying breath was only held. We felt
the afternoon turn over in its sleep
restless before it woke and blew us elsewhere
to practise separation like a scale
over and over until we run foolish,
to hoard and stroke the past till Now is gone,
to forget the past is now or not at all.

P. J. KAVANAGH

27

HOLLY

It rained when it should have snowed.
When we went to gather holly

the ditches were swimming, we were wet
to the knees, our hands were all jags

and water ran up our sleeves.
There should have been berries

but the sprigs we brought into the house
gleamed like smashed bottle-glass.

Now here I am, in a room that is decked
with the red-berried, waxy-leafed stuff,

and I almost forget what it's like
to be wet to the skin or longing for snow.

I reach for a book like a doubter
and want it to flare round my hand,

a black-letter bush, a glittering shield-wall
cutting as holly and ice.

SEAMUS HEANEY

LAMP

The lamp is needful in Spring, still,
Though the jar of daffodils
Outsplendours lamplight and hearthflames.

In summer, only near midnight
Is match struck to wick.
A moth, maybe, troubles the rag of flame.

Harvest. The lamp in the window
Summons the scythe-men.
A school-book lies on the sill, two yellow halves.

In December the lamp's a jewel,
The hearth ingots and incense.
A cold star travels across the pane.

GEORGE MACKAY BROWN

CHRISTMAS

Despite the forecast's promise,
It didn't snow that night;
But in the morning, flakes began
To glide all right.
Not enough to cover roads
Or even hide the grass;
But enough to change the light.

BERNARD O'DONOGHUE

TORTOISESHELLS OVERWINTERING

In my bedroom ceiling's shadiest corner
   a dark encampment of inverted tents
is sitting out the tyranny of Winter.

Like Israelites that keep God's covenants
   in sober arks, or nomad Bedouins
who hide rich mats in fustian tenements,

they fold the magic carpets of their wings,
   concealing hieroglyphics of the meadow
clapped between tatter-bordered coverings.

As dingy as the withered nettlebed,
   as drab as marbled bibles, charred by fire,
or chips of bark or stone, they could be dead

but hang by wiry legs, as fine as hair,
   close-clustered near the plaster desert's edge
like a proscribed religious sect at prayer.

This bivouac preserves the Summer's page
   during eclipse of dandelions and daisies;
it bears pressed sparks of sun through this dark age:

one night between oasis and oasis.

ANNA ADAMS

THE CENTIPEDE

In one brilliant moment there is your own soul's breath
searing in baby flesh
and dipping into curious things,
puddles and leaves.

A small hand is gripping your finger,
pulling you into the garden,
where the blossom he taps to see the snowy flutter
is that entranced moment that lasts beyond life
and might have come before it: an infinite
moment that waited for its entrance here.

Dig – dig here. He shows you a centipede –
the vital lightning, a single flame
of gold he's never seen before.

And neither, you realise, have you.
What the something is that fills your nothingness
is not his showing you how to dig,
but how to love.

GLYN HUGHES

SHEPHERDS

Night of the black moon.
Above the house, Venus
bright as a lamp.
The field glitters in the flashlight
with the thirty stars of their eyes.

Somewhere the croak of a bird
and far off, chained
in the yard of a nameless farm
a dog barks. Downwind
the smoke of our dying fire.

In the unsteady light of the torch
you shoulder the bale, break it,
ram the racks with the needling sweetness
of nettlescents, herbs, the trapped breath
of thirteen kinds of summer grasses.

The ewes are pushy,
Blackface first to the bucket,
then the one who hooves our shoulders
to hurry the mumble
of our iron hands.

You call from the dark –
first lambs steaming in lamplight.
We carry them in, one each, hot and yolky
with their strange scent of the sea,
the ewe in a panic at our heels.

Above us in the Square of Pegasus
a satellite wavers
like a torch in a field.

GILLIAN CLARKE

THE PATTERN

Thirty-six years, to the day, after our wedding
When a cold figure-revealing wind blew against you
And lifted your veil, I find in its fat envelope
The six-shilling *Vogue* pattern for your bride's dress,
Complicated instructions for stitching bodice
And skirt, box pleats and hems, tissue-paper outlines,
Semblances of skin which I nervously unfold
And hold up in snow light, for snow has been falling
On this windless day, and I glimpse your wedding dress
And white shoes outside in the transformed garden
Where the clothesline and every twig have been covered.

MICHAEL LONGLEY

OUR PEAR-TREE

In-
side
its actual shape
you can see
the one intended:
a semi-sphere rests squarely
on a trunk that's vertical.
Moving upwards
like a ladder
the lower branches are arranged symmetrically
in equidistant diagonals.
A partridge, greatly satisfied by its place
in the scheme of things,
sits plumb
in the middle
of the down-most 'V',
surrounded plentifully on all sides
by pears that hang like huge droplets, so ripe and golden
you'd think a child had painted them.
Thereafter
the design grows hectic, unpredictable.
Layers have been added, year by year,
in styles that aren't compatible – the media mixed, the details
all out of proportion.
In tempera,
nesting comfortably on branches naively strong enough to hold them,
are seven fat geese – concentrating hard (with fixed expressions) on egg-laying.
Higher up, and toppling, a noisy menagerie is bickering
over five gold rings,
boldly crayoned in.
Around and between, in a tangle of bendy twigs,
eight swans are clearly not a-swimming, though they are in water-colour,
and the leaves they're sitting on (in a spirit of compromise)
have turned blue and rippling.
Beyond the outermost, uppermost fringes, it's a Chagall fantasy:
twelve ladies dancing with eleven lords a-leaping
are swirling round and round the tree, in a blur of bluey-purple, twisted together
like interlocking coils or springs,
stretching their arms toward a bigger circle that's forever spiralling
in a hemisphere beyond our imagining, with stars and moons and planets hovering.
Evidently, it's in serious need of pruning.
But let's agree to leave our tree just as it is –
dishevelled, cacophonous, anarchic, cornucopian.
After all, you never know
what the
new year
will bring.

LUCY NEWLYN

ADVENT: GREENWICH REACH

Peace?

Watch the cormorant
making minute adjustment
to the angle of her inky,
solar-powered wings.

Joy?

Just beyond the boatyard
where abandoned burnt steel keels
into the mud, I met three kings
resting on their journey west
(yolk-yellow brocade, immaculate,
velvet, red as wine).

Goldfinches rattling the dry grasses,
wise to their gifts of seed.

Goodwill to Men?

The crane-driver is an artist. We enjoy
nodding acquaintance. His silver teeth flash,
gnawing at the coaster's narrow hold;
spitting, casual as a taster of fine wines,
a perfect pyramid of broken stones.
Until he spots me cycle up, holds
this huge everything quite still,
arced to perfection for a while.
He thumbs me through. I turn and watch.
His jaw drops with a smile.

JULIAN MAY

from PUMPKINS

Pulled up by a whole sunsplashed
field, I stood there covetous
to touch, skins,
                    drums
rhythmic, tumbled,
fullness of flesh
                    on withered haulms,
the raw energy of the earth made visible
and when it rains,
a sea of sailors in yellow oils.

SALLY FESTING

37

PRIMA NIX

for the nuns of Fetlar

First snow
not yet dashed with a hare's foot.
We could go to our graves in white
not dead
but simply listening.

A simple interior,
the sound of the sea
through snowfall,
a cross-shaped cut in the membrane
behind the lens.

Prayer without words;
where the light meets the water
great areas left
unprinted
like a Japanese rice-paper painting.

Salt settles on the skin.
The ghostly disciples let
their heads fall forward
in the wind
like melancholy thistles.

Our Lady of the Isles
all the blues swallow one another.
Christ colours the quickbread.
The islands glide
into one body.

PAULINE STAINER

EMPRESS SADAKO CONSIDERS SNOW

When I wore my hair
straight across my forehead,
I loved deep drifts
in my father's yard.
We would spend all day
making a snow mountain,
praying to Goddess Shirayama
not to let it melt.
Now I stir the red embers
in my brazier, watching flurries
through the icy lattice
and have ordered that no one
disturb the snow outside my rooms
by shuffling wooden clogs there
or heaping it into a silly mountain.
Snow is shapeliest when left alone.

JULIE O'CALLAGHAN

UNDER THE AVALANCHE

I've heard that a pocket of air
  can save your life

so I'm hunkering down in the grey
  darkness of snow

and pulling cold around me
  like a quilt.

I'm warming the tiny air
  in front of my face

re-breathing my own hot breath . . .

as if I were already
  home and dry

reading under the bedclothes
  with a torch.

CATHERINE BYRON

```
goodk kkkkk unjam ingwe nches l a s s?  start again goodk
lassw enche sking start again kings t a r t! again sorry
goodk ingwe ncesl ooked outas thef?  unmix asloo kedou
tonth effff rewri tenow goodk ingwe ncesl asloo kedou
tonth effff fffff unjam feast ofsai ntste venst efanc
utsai ntrew ritef easto fstep toeso rryan dsons orry!
start again good? yesgo odkin gwenc eslas looke dout?
doubt wrong track start again goodk ingwe ncesl asloo
kedou tonth efeas tofst ephph phphp hphph unjam phphp
repea tunja mhphp scrub carol hphph repea tscru bcaro
lstop subst itute track merry chris tmasa ndgoo dnewy
earin 1699? check digit banks orryi n1966 endme ssage
```

EDWIN MORGAN

CHRISTMAS IN ENVELOPES

Monks are at it again, quaffing, carousing;
And stage-coaches, cantering straight out of Merrie England,
In a flurry of whips and fetlocks, sacks and Santas.

Raphael has been roped in, and Botticelli;
Experts predict a vintage year for Virgins.

From the theologically challenged, Richmond Bridge,
Giverny, a lugger by moonlight, doves.   Ours

Costs less than these in money, more in time;
Like them, is hopelessly irrelevant,
But brings, like them, the essential message

love

U. A. FANTHORPE

SKATER

Score your wild music, though the sedge
blackens at the brackish edge
and tales of tanglewood and leaf
rehearse what comes, and comes to grief.
Let snow and rain kick over traces,
plash down devices, airs and graces
to lost features on lost faces
and sullen landscapes waterishly
ponder their loss of memory.
Cut bolder figures; hold your sway,
ride the bright slip-stream of your day.

PETER SCUPHAM

LISTENING

The wind's listening, and the rain on Whirlaw,
and the valley's long shadows in the evening.

A late blackbird breaks in on the quiet
of moss and lichen, and I know I'm here.

The trees know I'm here, and someone else
knows I'm here, listening, as I'm listening.

It seems like myself, only older, stranger,
knowing I'm not really the little boy I am.

HERBERT LOMAS

WEAVERS

Scalloway, Shetland, December 2002

He's there as I walk out to Port Arthur,
still there when I come back,
an old man eager to catch my eye
in the bright bay of his nursing-home.

This lone figure had not brought me here,
that was the work of December light
condensing the treeless landscape,
but as Scalloway fades it is he who lingers.

Cradling in his arms the same stool
my silent uncle had made. Matched guardians
of an unearthed memory, disturbed by its returning,
both waving because one had never spoken.

DAVID KEEFE

'WOULD THEY HAD STAY'D'

1

The colour of meadow hay, with its meadow-sweet
And liver-spotted dock leaves, they were there
Before we spotted them, all eyes and evening,
Up to their necks in the meadow.
       'Where? I still—'
'There.'
  'Oh yes. Oh God, yes. Lovely.'
         And they didn't
Move away.
     There, like the air on hold.
The step of light on grass, halted mid-light.
Heartbeat and pupil. A match for us. And watching.

2

Norman MacCaig, come forth from the deer of Magdalen,
Those startlers standing still in fritillary land,
Heather-sentries far from the heath. Be fawn
To the redcoat, gallowglass in the Globe,
Tidings of trees that walked and were seen to walk.

3

Sorley MacLean. A mirage. A stag on a ridge
In the western desert above the burnt-out tanks.

4

What George Mackay Brown saw was a drinking deer
That glittered by the water. The human soul
In mosaic. Wet celandine and ivy.
Allegory hard as Earl Rognvald's shield
Polished until its undersurface surfaced
Like peat smoke mulling through Byzantium.

SEAMUS HEANEY

'HEUREUX QUI, COMME ULYSSE . . . '

Happy he (or she)
Who travels the day
Hopefully, and the
World without hope, calm,
A smiling stoic
Who savours what his
Life may bring. Happy
The day of birth, and
Happy our dying:
Without it, life will
Not be known. Let all
Be seen for itself,
For what it is! Do
Not fear the voyage
Towards the world's edge
And the final hour.
Take pity on time.
Welcome each event
Because it greets you
As the destined one.

EDWARD LUCIE-SMITH

NEWS FROM NORFOLK

The arrowhead of geese
   labours
 into the wind as they
    tug on their
      rope of sky
    honking as they go.

  One falls to feed
then another
   then a third
    the flock tumbling
like
  fridge alphabet letters

   or a broken string
of pearls.

CAROLINE GILFILLAN

RICHARD LONG'S *BUZZARD*

From high soaring on thermals
The tame buzzard lays a flight path
Straight down through the paddock
To the bare oak:

This shallow trench line
Filled with Norfolk flint –
Shards, knuckles, yellow-white bones,
What remains of us.

TONY CURTIS

ON SEEING A CHRISTIAN GARDENER AT EIGHTY

Three days to Christmas – a mild
Bright westerly morning.
He is on his spry old knees
Preparing a spring bed,

A kind of active prayer,
His manger for the child.
And time may give him warning
That soon he will not be there;

He will not heed.
Beliefs can coalesce
In star and seed to wake
The living and the dead;

My unbeliever's eye
Beholds a practical
Reverence all can share
In face of a miracle.

PATRIC DICKINSON

EVE

And then, they say, no spirit dares stir abroad.

We've left the dark to its own devices, fairylights
twinkling-by-numbers on the blind side of curtains,
the bobbing orange marsh-fire of a Santa
looming across the fields. They've barred the church

against the last post-pub conversions
spilling the dregs of mulled carols.
The air's been cleared of its ghosts,

so what is blowing out
is just itself now,

the night before.

MATTHEW FRANCIS

DAWN

Dawn lay
Mother of pearl
Below the rooftops.

Trees
In purple robes
Lined their avenues.

Mists pillowed
The hills like
Quiet sheep.

Without lifting
A finger, light
Unlocked the gardens.

Window panes
Glistened in dew
When day breathed on them.

Something like glory
Hung all over
The air.

RICHARD BURNS

HYACINTHS

The tortoise earth seems to have stopped dead.
Certainly the trees are dead, their limbs
Are broken, we can hear them clattering.
It must be about the midpoint. Last year
At this time you knelt for the hyacinths.

You brought them in like bread, in fired bowls,
From secret ovens of darkness. Three or four rooms
Soon had a column and a birth. Pictures show
The crib shining similarly
When Christ flowered from Mary the bulb.

The Kings stand warming their hands on the light.
Their gifts are nothing by comparison.
I suppose they feared that without some miracle,
Without the light and the bread of hyacinths,
The earth would never nudge forward out of the dark.

DAVID CONSTANTINE

from CAEDMON

That night frost stretched
the fields into stiff white sheets;
from post, strut and roof glinting
ice-fingers pointed to the ground.
But within walls, reed-woven,
mud-baked, we warded off
the wind-beast's bellow and bite.
Herded in the wool of our own warmth,
near red-gold flames that licked
logs, then leapt to find the hole
to heaven, we defeated winter's pikes.
That festive night we filled
our bodies' troughs with roasted meats,
with mead that honeys the senses, muzzes
the mind. As ever I kept quiet,
stoked myself with the comfort rising
from the rush-strewn floor, the goodwill
steaming through talk and laughter.

MYRA SCHNEIDER

DECEMBER 25TH, 12 NOON

No, honestly, we are more organised than we look.
The piles of clothes are all washed.
I have fed the birds, then the cats,
Now the cats are out: catching birds,
It starts to unravel. The cream will not whip,
It mocks the whisk in white hissing waves.
The cat flies the long grass, scattering wings,
The creased pale blouses shiver and fall.
Time, I think, to drink, then wander
The flooded footpaths, to waver and call
And Christmas, and Merry, and to you all.

ALISON BRACKENBURY

EAVESDROPPING

4 a.m.
and the swifts
over the house in the disappearing
dark, the swifts open-mouthed, ten,
twenty of them, thirty swifts now
and in every open-mouthed swift I picture
a heart the size of a hawthorn berry,
blood red to bursting those swift hearts,
thirty hearts in thirty swifts
over the house this morning where I stand
naked at the window, listening to my own heart –
perhaps the closest I will get to prayer –
and eavesdropping on the silence of the morning
where every swift is a black new moon
upon the black mosque of the air.

ROBERT MINHINNICK

THE HEART-IN-WAITING

Jesus walked through whispering wood:
'I am pale blossom, I am blood berry,
I am rough bark, I am sharp thorn.
This is the place where you will be born.'

Jesus went down to the skirl of the sea:
'I am long reach, I am fierce comber,
I am keen saltspray, I am spring tide.'
He pushed the cup of the sea aside

And heard the sky which breathed-and-blew:
'I am the firmament, I am shape-changer,
I cradle and carry and kiss and roar,
I am infinite roof and floor.'

All day he walked, he walked all night,
Then Jesus came to the heart at dawn.
'Here and now,' said the heart-in-waiting,
'This is the place where you must be born.'

KEVIN CROSSLEY-HOLLAND

ROUND

JOHN FULLER

NATIVITY

One topic throughout the whole of Bethlehem tonight:
money – and the tyranny of Caesar Augustus.

But there are a variety of antidotes.

To mock the poor
(beggar, leper, lunatic)
who point and wildly cry
at the latest comet in the sky.

To hear your horoscope read by a wise man.

To run to the camp-fires
and dance and kiss through Saturnalia.

To enjoy a sly joke about King Herod.

Or, swaddled in cheap wine,
to follow the star of lust to its warm conclusion
in the straw of some unoccupied stall.

Angel, animal . . . impossible to distinguish.

Only that cry is recognisably shaped –
and then, the smirk of gold,
a shepherd's question mark,
the ingenuous slobber of a fatted calf
playing counterpoint
to the Christ child's first feed.

All believe, as yet, that they are here
to enjoy these riches:
this sweet and phosphorous manure,
the warmth, a mother's milk.

JOHN GREENING

THE THORN

There was no berry on the bramble
only the thorn,
there was no rose, not one petal,
only the bare thorn
the night he was born.

There was no voice to guide them,
only the wind's whistling,
there was no light in the stable,
only the starshine
and a candle guttering
the night he was born.

From nothing and nowhere
this couple came,
at every border
their papers were wrong
but they reached the city
and begged for a room.

There was no berry on the bramble,
no rose, not one petal,
only the thorn,
and a cold wind whispering
the night he was born.

HELEN DUNMORE

A SLOVAK CHRISTMAS TREE

Above the altar floats the Christ Child;
Rosy, plump, baroque he floats free
From the round breasts of the Virgin Mary
Who is all, as they claim here, 'blood and milk'.
He floats in shimmering blue and gold
Beneath the branches of a gaunt tree.

Outside the church we wrap our natures
Against the cold wind and the snow.
Unleaved, linden, ash and beech show
The crookedness the Christ Child endures
From us; bare branches snow-blurred
That the cold wind creaks to and fro.

The Christ Child will burst his rosy bud
To the everlasting green of leaves,
But he'll be fruit for our unbelief
On a gaunt tree whose wood stains red
As each year our sins bud, leaf and shed
While we claim, disclaim, proclaim belief.

JAMES SUTHERLAND-SMITH

61

CHRISTMAS ROSÉ

Copernicus would have named
constellations after its
dot-to-dot fizz.

Pinball on the tongue,
like the anticipatory chatter
in a theatre.

See-through, taste-through,
a high octave chill
in fishnet tights,

All lips and no shoulders.
Sweet pretending to be *brut*,
a very brigand of a wine.

MICHAEL HENRY

PROMISE

Remember, the time of year
when the future appears
like a blank sheet of paper
a clean calendar, a new chance.
On thick white snow

you vow fresh footprints
then watch them go
with the wind's hearty gust.
So fill your glass. Here's tae us. Promises
made to be broken, made to last.

JACKIE KAY

ORANGES AT CHRISTMAS TIME

I can see our dining-room still,
the sideboard with a central mirror,
heavy two-handled fruit bowl
doubled by its own reflection
in the glass; round red Jonathans
polished to perfection, Jaffa oranges
and sometimes pears; no rules
forbidding us to touch – they were
there for the picking.

At Christmas there were tangerines
for eating at the table after meals.
A conniving uncle taught us how to spit
the pips backwards into the fire
without getting up from our chairs,
my mother indulgent to his goings-on.
He was the same uncle who tickled us
till we screamed for mercy then drew
breath to ask for more.

Last Christmas I was given a tree,
a Citrus Mitis, fragrant with flowers
growing in clusters, perfectly formed,
delicate and white, five small oranges
appearing at the same time. They
ripened to perfection and I used
them in my next batch of marmalade,
alongside the Sevilles and the limes,
and it tasted fine.

New oranges upon my tree this year,
rich colour set to rhythm and to rhyme,
their succulence a secret learned
in childhood, schooled by my mother's
tolerance – acceptance of the aunt who
taught us to suck oranges messily
through a sugar lump, thrust deep into
a hole made through the rind, to reach
the flesh beneath.

Oranges at Christmas time, memory
sharp as their flavour, sweet as the
indulgences of childhood and the lasting
power of love.

ELIZABETH BEWICK

MARY'S CAROL

Why do you give the baby gold?
The guiding star foretold a king.
A little child shall lead you, bring
No metal rich and cold.

Who brings my boy this frankincense?
The star foretold a priestly role.
A little child shall save your soul,
Not gifts of great expense.

What is this myrrh? What do you see?
The star foretold a bitter cup.
'And I if I be lifted up
Shall draw all men to me.'

A child shall lead you from tonight.
The angel heralded his birth.
Our Saviour born to save the earth,
Our Way, our Truth, our Light.

Three gifts that far outweigh all gold
And gifts like frankincense and myrrh.
Sleep, child, my little comforter,
That no star has foretold.

PETER DALE

WINTER WINGS

Wymondham Abbey

How brilliantly the sun
for a moment strides
through the glass
then hides
in deep
recesses
in the very aisles
it so briefly caresses,

so the heart stops and restarts
without noticing
it has stopped:
a swing
lurching,
an eye lost
in mid-blink, dark birds
in full-flight, swimming through dust.

GEORGE SZIRTES

ST ITA'S LULLABY

Hush my sweet Jesus, hush my little lamb
Lamps are being lit in Killeedy
Footsteps are failing, the sun's sinking down.

Hush my sweet Jesus, hush my little lamb
Streams hug their beds near Killeedy
The straw in the barns is fragrant and warm.

Hush my sweet Jesus, hush my little lamb
The wind falls asleep in Killeedy
The moon's dissolving and the night is calm.

Hush my sweet Jesus, hush my little lamb
Angels descend on Killeedy
A snowfall of stars until the new dawn.

Hush my sweet Jesus, hush my little lamb
Hush, hush, hush . . .

JAMES HARPUR

SPEAKING OF ANGELS

I don't believe in angels
(even when I can see them lined up more than fifty feet

above my head
back to back in pairs as if uncertain about what's to be or not)

I'm quite impervious
to the pale curtains they wear for dresses, their gold-plate

haloes and curls
and bedtime-story wings like quattrocento Disney

supposed to make you
trust the status of their prequels and special announcements

The ones above me now
I can see by the clerestory's falling light were once spangled

in red and green and silver –
so high up they escaped Cromwell's lads on the rampage in
      1644

and I will admit to
their faded wooden charms . . . but the kind of inspired uttering

I can take more happily
on trust comes from the crafty player of a baryton

that's like a rare enhanced viol
a cello look-alike with secret strings whose plucked notes as
      well as bowed

tell me something
more persuasive, not to say heavenly, from their steel and gut –

that what's most sublime
is what's most human, soaring right up to the startled angels

and beyond,
their wings outstretched like transfixed fliers

(say, silver-streaked
hawk moths or some other casual migrants)

as if unable
to resist this awkward truth but still gaping in disbelief

RODNEY PYBUS

68

THE SIBYLS IN AMIENS CATHEDRAL

Thin-waisted Gothic sibyls
with pale calm faces
under wimples of clean Flanders linen,
holding your classical
attributes in elegant
fingers: the book,
the palm, the sword, the scroll,
images eaten
away and fading back
into the flaking
painted plaster and stone.

I can just distinguish which
is the Delphic one,
the Libyan, the Cumaean,
though your look and style
are those of later days,
Christian times,
your colours the gold and blue
of chapel banners,
soft madder-pink and red
of hawthorn flowers,
lush Somme-river green.

Your sister, the Tiburtine,
told Augustus
of Christ's coming, and so,
as oracles
of his triumph, on these cathedral
walls you stand
with the Prophets – proud pagan women,
half forgotten:
like the message you brought once,
but long ago,
to troubled northern souls.

RUTH FAINLIGHT

MITHRAS AND THE MILKMAN

Mithras Lord of the Sun has killed the bull,
The soldiers praise him.
In the North-East he stopped the wall of wind.
Upon Thames' banks he carved the muddy cave.
The soldiers praised him

Who stole him from the Persians. On the way
His red-hot birth was dulled to Christmas Day.

On Boxing Day the milkman sails through dark.
Whine of the motor cuts inside his head.
He lost his wife, a son and several teeth,
My note 'Two, please'. Three pints crash down instead.
I wake in sweat, wrestle through tangled sheets.
He climbs the cab's hot cave. The bull is dead.

ALISON BRACKENBURY

BEAGLES

That Boxing Day morning, I would hear the familiar, far-
   off gowls and gulders
over Keenaghan and Aughanlig
of a pack of beagles, old dogs disinclined to chase a car
   suddenly quite unlike
themselves, pups coming helter-skelter
across the plowlands with all the chutzpah of veterans
of the trenches, their slate-grays, cinnamons, liver-
   browns, lemons, rusts and violets
turning and twisting, unseen, across the fields,
their gowls and gulders turning and twisting after the
   twists and turns
of the great hare who had just now sauntered into the yard
   where I stood on tiptoe
astride my new Raleigh cycle,
his demeanor somewhat louche, somewhat lackadaisical
under the circumstances, what with him standing on
   tiptoe
as if to mimic me, standing almost as tall as I, looking as
   if he might for a moment put
himself in my place, thinking better of it, sloping off
   behind the lorry-bed.

PAUL MULDOON

71

AN AUSTRIAN CHRISTMAS

These few cold peaks, a lyric verse, a name,
and *Eine Kleine* in the coffee shop.
Vienna boys grow ears of purest grain,
whose music is the one unfattening crop
in this petite state. Slender resources
were forced to folds and whirls and creamy heights
by pressures from within, until psychosis.
And now, from a green couch, the mountain shouts
out Bruckner, the lake ringing Strauss, Strauss, Strauss,
as Schubert's hidden mill-stream fights the freeze
and Mozart avalanches the opera house,
Haydn goes on trimming Christmas trees
like Joseph when the angel first arrives . . .
All dream of warmth and youth kicking dry leaves.

JOHN GREENING

SUNT LACRIMAE RERUM

The glittering dance of brilliants must be strung
On that dark thread of sadness which is time,
No matter what bright melodies are sung.

When great symphonic combers swell and climb
Then curl and, swooping, rush towards the shore,
We hear a faint and melancholy chime.

This might come from a drowned cathedral or
Be carried on the wind from inland tower
In market-place, or church on distant moor.

Beneath the surging glory and the power
Of Beethoven or Bach, or tenderness
Of Schubert lieder's frailer sonic flower

We hear the spectral sighing of distress,
For time is music's element and we
Know murderous time can offer no redress.

Yet which of us, I wonder, were he free
To choose, would wish away the voice that sings
The keening descant of mortality

Inseparable from all that music brings
Of love, heart-piercing truth, the tears in things.

VERNON SCANNELL

CHILDERMAS

Enjoy your Christmas sitting by the fire
replete with interactive fantasy,
eyes flickering but focused on screen where
warriors brandish blades and victims flee.
There's little fear of an angelic choir
to break the wintry silence. Press a key:
relish your first night huddled in a byre
before you learn to be a refugee.

Out of this world it is, an unreal toy
better than TV news or old pretence:
for every three wise guys who come with joy
and gifts of gold and myrrh and frankincense
out of the east to greet the glory boy,
one Herod slaughters many innocents.

PAUL HYLAND

AT THE PANTOMIME

Yes, it was great to laugh
When one of the ugly sisters thought she was more beautiful
Than her other half,
And it was fun to cheer
When out of the magic lantern with a puff of smoke
We saw the genie appear,
And it was time to weep
When Snow White bit into the shiny apple
Or Beauty pricked her finger and fell asleep,
And it was really good
When the Prince arrived to wake them up
Though of course we knew that he would,
But best of all
When the villain sneaked on
(And, no, we didn't really want him to be gone)
It was absolute bliss
To hiss!

JOHN MOLE

NEWTON'S NOTEBOOK (1667)

For 3 Prisms	*0. 3. 0*
For keeping Christmas	*0. 5. 0*
Lost at cards at twist	*0. 15. 0*
At y^e Tavern severally	*1. 0. 0*

Three kings in succession
and bust again!
This season the sky's alive
and leads to the tavern –
no bed unwarmed,
the last room taken.

In the beginning
light split like a plaything
of little winged rainbows
and I sought
something to bring it
together again.

My birthday and His
on its planetary return:
the chimney roaring,
the jug half spilt,
the maid with her arms full
at the clattering door.

All this and the great
experiment
of God dividing Himself,
Logos to locus.
And the babe with his pippin cheeks
tumbled to earth.

STUART HENSON

ANGEL

Bellini's *Virgin and Child*

Her child at
the edge of the world;
wild, dense.

He looks down,
his first landscape
immense

with dark pines,
lines of warriors,
frowns.

She holds him,
her large hands,
long fingers

folding
his soft
belly.

Lingering there
they are silent,
ordinary

but he belongs
in air now,
a cherub

perching.
She launches him
through bird songs,

his auburn hair
curly as smoke
over ruined towns.

VERNON HALE

OUR LADY OF INDIGO

Desultory blue –
the weight of water,
scarcely a blue animal
on the ark.

Blue to conjure with –
fields of blue alfalfa
making the moonlight
something else.

Profound blue –
the master of the blue crucifix
opening his throat
to her thin-blue milk.

PAULINE STAINER

GOD'S IMAGE

So matter of fact. Casual
as the undreamed-of
un-birthday gift. Unwrapped,
disarming; an act
of faith simple

as the wheel. As if love
were everyday, unassuming
and certain of return:
left hand answering
to right in a rough

arc, tentative as living;
a point of rest.
Such trust is matchless –
look, his hands are pinned
to stop his giving.

JANE GRIFFITHS

HAPPY EVERYDAY

All days are created equal.
Everyday has the right to recognition
And no day should be subject to
Cruel or degrading treatment.
Everyday has the right to freedom of expression
And the right to participate
In the cultural life of the community.
Everyday has the right to belong to
The religion of its choice,
And should not suffer discrimination based on
Sunshine, rainfall, temperature,
Or seasonal orientation.

BENJAMIN ZEPHANIAH

BIRD PSALM

The Swallow said,
He comes like me,
Longed for; unexpectedly.

The superficial eye
Will pass him by,
Said the Wren.

The best singer ever heard.
No one will take much notice,
Said the Blackbird.

The Owl said,
He is who, who is he
Who enters the heart as soft
As my soundless wings, as me.

U. A. FANTHORPE

81

FLIGHT INTO EGYPT

Some, who were warned in dreams to pack and go,
trekked for a line drawn in the stupid sand;
found scrub and mirage at the rainbow's end,
the tombs of strangers in occluding snow
and unmade promises in promised land.

Trapped in the cruel nonsenses of things,
some found the guiding star a marker-flare
which drew more darkness down upon their fear;
died by their neighbours' knives, or bladed wings
whirling new plagues about the ice-blue air.

And Innocence, which lived a day, and died,
sighs in the ebb-voice of a broken wave
how this one child was cupboarded by love
until his flesh grew ripe, then crucified
by those whose childhood was an open grave.

PETER SCUPHAM

A FAGGOT

The fig, our nakedness before the fire.
Blackthorn, the spite – a thin smoke.
Hazel, your finger on the deep pulse.
Oak, the heartwood.
Ash, a staff.
Beech, like a stone in two.
Yew, a sustainable sorrow.
The reed, answer to the storm.
O cedar – O my Lebanon!
Ivy, the green in winter.
Willow, the wand in the rune.
Holly, a birth – the spark in the fire.
Juniper, the fragrance.
Sycamore, the brittle rung.
Briar – anger anger anger.
The blood of the one who binds the faggot.
Viburnum, the flower of winter.
I bid them all burn –
Oh, and a wild rose –
A happy New Year.

JOHN MOAT

NEW YEAR

The cleared hillside paler in the winter's day,
The fire melting now, single, a sobered glare:

The tangle and dead-weight are lifted away;
Stray song of birds ornaments the leafless air.

ROBERT WELLS

TRACKING

The New Year rolls in on a cloud
that turns the world like a white page.
In the cold snow-light of the day we read
the narratives of the hours of night:
the journeyings of fox, cat, rabbit, badger,
each with its twists, its evasions,
its doubling-back.

And as we return, wrapped up in our scarves
and hoods, like nursery creatures
that lost and found themselves in the wood,
we're amused by the prints of the story so far
and the fields of the future closed
like an uncut book.

STUART HENSON

CHRISTMAS CARDS

Slip through the letter box with messages:
Some bland, some more intense, some aching with
Bereavements, wives abandoned, loss of jobs.

The annual contact on a patient card.
'See you next year' some say and quite forget
Before the ink is dry. A plaster patch

That leaves no sticky mark on minor wounds
However much the cover faces please
With coloured art or kitsch or nearly art.

One threatens every time in wiry script
'This is the last card I shall send. I am
Too old now'. Still it slides into my hand.

And there is one that comes anonymous,
Unsigned, the postmark adds its mystery,
A smudge, a ghost behind this paper mask?

Perhaps there'll be a few to tuck away
After the show, in an old envelope,
Fingered at times because the sender once

Carved hope into a fraction of your years;
Or others will imply 'I am still here' –
A comma on your page a life ago.

LOTTE KRAMER

NEW YEAR'S DAY AT LEPE

Set out on a morning of white thaw
smoking between oaks, Hatchet pond so still
it might have been frozen
except for the long slender rods
as if painted on its dark blue glaze.
Saw nothing of the *Private, Keep Out*
notices of semi-feudal estates,
but cock pheasants in brown fields
of sharp-edged clods, poking out their necks.
Then the small rusty bell of the shingle
tinkled and grated as it dragged,
a shadowy tanker bared its round stern
and Marchwood power station exhaled
a breath which the sun tinged pink;
but of all things none seemed newer
than gravel with its sheen of fresh oranges
at the water's lip. Brought away that,
and an old transparent moon
over the Island, the delicate industrial sky
blue-grey as a herring gull's back,
and a small sunny boy running beside
the great wet novelty shouting *wasser, wasser.*

JEREMY HOOKER

BLUEBELL TIME

Out where the new leaf gives a warm colour
bluebells are the botanonym of cool.
On hot days we want to stop and drink from them
like marathon runners.

For something stronger the poison bottle blue
of nightshade, for something more fugitive
the monk's hood blue of aconite.

Out in the deep: viridian and oxide
of chromium. Where shadow
darkens the palette, we breathe in
the powder of blue.

For something richer the royal blue
of iris. For something gentler
the naive blue of cornflower.

And so to bluebells. Like portraits
of long-forgotten winners from the past
when the year moves on to lilies. And to roses.

MICHAEL HENRY

RAIN

wh
en
t
he
r
ai   w
n   e
is   ar
f   e
al   in
li   cl
ng   in
i   ed
n   t
lo   o
ng   fo
c   rg
ol   et
um   w
ns   ha
t
a
mi
ra
cl
e
it
i
s.

GEORGE MacBETH

PEREDELKINO

He told them everything became
miraculous:
        a snowfall in the trees

or how a bird sings to a single
streetlamp

        at the far end of a road
between the churchyard and the city square.

He spoke of miracles as casually
as others speak of memory or time

so when he left them there
            at winter's end
they dressed him in his father's suit and shoes

and left the yard door open
            for the gift
of elsewhere:

        for the dark scent of the earth
that claims us with such unexpected

tenderness
        we know before the last
to take our leave as someone in a scarf

and winter coat might vanish in spring rain.

JOHN BURNSIDE

Bibliographical Note

The poems in *Light Unlocked* – or versions of them – first appeared in the following publications. Poems unpublished before their inclusion in this anthology are marked with an asterisk.

Anna Adams
'Tortoiseshells Overwintering', *Six Legs Good*, Mandeville Press 1987, then *A Paper Ark*, Peterloo 1996

Elizabeth Bewick
'Oranges at Christmas Time'*

Alison Brackenbury
'December 25th, 12 noon.'*
'Mithras and the Milkman', *Bricks and Ballads*, Carcanet 2004

Edwin Brock
'Snow', *And Another Thing*, Enitharmon Press 1999

Alan Brownjohn
'Summer Time Ends', *The Cat Without E-Mail*, Enitharmon Press 2001

Richard Burns
'Dawn', *Book With No Back Cover*, David Paul 2003

John Burnside
'Peredelkino'*

Catherine Byron
'Under the Avalanche', *The Way You Say the World*, Shoestring Press 2003

Gillian Clarke
'The Stone Hare'*
'Shepherds', *Making the Beds for the Dead*, Carcanet 2003

David Constantine
'Hyacinths', *Madder*, Bloodaxe Books 1987

Wendy Cope
'The Christmas Life', *If I Don't Know*, Faber 2001

Kevin Crossley-Holland
'The Heart-in-Waiting', *Selected Poems*, Enitharmon Press 2001

Tony Curtis
'Richard Long's *Buzzard*'*

Peter Dale
'Mary's Carol'*

Patric Dickinson
'On Seeing a Christian Gardener at Eighty', *A Rift in Time*, Chatto &
Windus/Hogarth Press 1982

Helen Dunmore
'The Thorn'*

Ruth Fainlight
'The Sybils in Amiens Cathedral', *Sybils and Others*, Hutchinson 1980

U. A. Fanthorpe
'Christmas in Envelopes' and 'Bird Psalm', *Christmas Poems*,
Enitharmon Press / Peterloo Poets 2001

Sally Festing
from *Pumpkins*'*

Matthew Francis
'Eve'*

John Fuller
'Round', *A Round of Carols* by Bryan Kelly, Royal School of Church
Music 1989

Rhian Gallagher
'The Annunciation', *Salt Water Creek*, Enitharmon Press 2003

Caroline Gilfillan
'News from Norfolk'*

John Greening
'Nativity'*
'An Austrian Christmas'*

Jane Griffiths
'God's Image'*

Vernon Hale
'Angel'*

James Harpur
'St Ita's Lullaby'*

Seamus Heaney
'Holly', *Station Island*, Faber 1984
'Would they had stay'd', *Electric Light*, Faber 2001

Michael Henry
'Christmas Rosé'*
'Bluebell Time'*

Stuart Henson
'Newton's Notebook (1667)'*
'Tracking'*

Jeremy Hooker
'New Year's Day at Lepe', *Solent Shore*, Carcanet 1974

Glyn Hughes
'The Centipede', *Dancing out of the Dark Side*, Shoestring Press 2005

Paul Hyland
'Childermas', *Art of the Impossible: New & Selected Poems 1974-2004*,
Bloodaxe Books 2004

P. J. Kavanagh
'Christmas Holiday', *One and One*, Heinemann 1960, then *Collected Poems*, Carcanet 1992

Jackie Kay
'Promise', *Life Mask*, Bloodaxe Books 2005

Judith Kazantzis
'Pages from *A Sussex Calendar*', *Swimming Through the Grand Hotel*,
Enitharmon Press 1997

David Keefe
'Weavers'*

Lotte Kramer
'Christmas Cards', *The Phantom Lane*, Rockingham Press 2000

Herbert Lomas
'Listening', *The Vale of Todmorden*, Arc Publications 2003

Michael Longley
'The Pattern', *Snow Water*, Cape 2004

Edward Lucie-Smith
'Heureux qui, comme Ulysse . . .', *Changing Shape: New & Selected
Poems*, Carcanet 2002

Hugh Lupton
'Cock Robin and Cutty Wren'*

George MacBeth
'Rain', Daedalus Poems (poem card), 2nd series, no. 11

George Mackay Brown
'House of Winter' and 'Lamp', *Collected Poems*, John Murray 2005

Julian May
'Advent: Greenwich Reach'*

Roger McGough
'The Dada Christmas Catalogue', *Lucky*, Viking 1993, Puffin 1994

Robert Minhinnick
'Eavesdropping'*

John Moat
'A Faggot', *100 Poems*, Phoenix Press 1998

John Mole
'Wings', *Counting the Chimes: New and Selected Poems 1975–2003*,
Peterloo Poets 2004
'At the Pantomime', *The Wonder Dish*, Oxford University Press 2002

Edwin Morgan
'The Computer's Second Christmas Card', *Collected Poems*, Carcanet
1990

Paul Muldoon
'Beagles', *Moy, Sand and Gravel*, Faber 2002

Lucy Newlyn
'Our Pear-Tree'*

Julie O'Callaghan
'Empress Sadako Considers Snow', Closet Press, Trinity College,
Dublin, 1984, then *What's What*, Bloodaxe Books 1991

Bernard O'Donoghue
'Christmas', *Here Nor There*, Chatto & Windus 1999

Rodney Pybus
'Speaking of Angels'*

Michael Symmons Roberts
'I feel the rush of Gabriel's wings', commissioned by King's College,
Cambridge, and BBC2 for *Carols from Kings* 2001, then published as
a pamphlet by Grand Phoenix Press 2002

Lawrence Sail
'The Glimmering'*

Carole Satyamurti
'Christmas Circulars', *Changing the Subject*, Oxford University Press
1990

Vernon Scannell
'Sunt Lacrimae Rerum', *Views and Distances*, Enitharmon Press 2000

Myra Schneider
from 'Caedmon', *Cathedral of Birds*, Littlewood/Giant Steps 1988, then
Insisting on Yellow, Enitharmon Press 2000

Peter Scupham
'Skater'*
'Flight into Egypt', *Oxford Poets 2001: an Anthology*, Carcanet 2001

Matt Simpson
'Fragment', *Getting There*, Liverpool University Press 2001

Pauline Stainer
'Prima Nix', *Parable Island*, Bloodaxe Books 1999
'Our Lady of Indigo'*

Anne Stevenson
'Carol of the Birds', *A Report from the Border*, Bloodaxe Books 2003

James Sutherland-Smith
'A Slovak Christmas Tree'*

George Szirtes
'Winter Wings', *Reel*, Bloodaxe Books 2004

Robert Wells
'New Year'*

Rowan Williams
'Advent Calendar', *The Poems of Rowan Williams*, Perpetua Press 2002

Benjamin Zephaniah
'Happy Everyday', British Council calendar